Stranded in Sub-Atomica

Tim Turnbull was born in North Yorkshire in 1960 and now lives in Scotland.

Also by Tim Turnbull

Work
What was that?

Stranded in Sub-Atomica
Tim Turnbull

Donut Press

Published by Donut Press in 2005.

Donut Press, PO Box 45093,
London, N4 1UZ.
www.donutpress.co.uk

Printed and bound by G&B Printers,
Unit 4, Mount Road Industrial Estate,
Mount Road, Feltham, Middlesex,
TW13 6AR.

Donut Press gratefully acknowledges
the support of Andrew Mitchell
Consulting, Arts Council England,
Business Link for London,
Collage Arts and Prevista.

ISBN: 0954198360

for Shiona

Acknowledgements are due to the editors of the following publications in which some of these poems first appeared: *Artefiction* (Stride, 2000), *www.barcelonareview.com*, *The Illustrated Ape*, *Lie of the Land* (P&K, 2004), *Magma, Matter, The New Formalist, New Writing Scotland 23* (ASLS, 2005), *Oral* (Sceptre, 1999), *www.thepoem.co.uk*, *The Printer's Devil, www.shu.ac.uk/proof, Reactions*[5] (Pen & Inc, 2005), *Rialto, Rising, The Slab, Ten Hallam Poets* (Mews Press, 2005), *www.thundersandwich.com*, *Wordwrights* and *Wozu Vögul, Bücher, Jazz* (Wunderhorn, 2005).

Contents

Stranded in Sub-Atomica

Badlands

We wake up on the floor of a council house
in Cumbria, feeling a bit sick. Everywhere
smells of oil and leather. Out on the road
a neat row of Triumphs and Kawasakis.

The daylight is nasty but in the kitchen
there's coffee. Carol makes anaemic toast
and hands it round. John comes down from the room
he shares with Carol's eldest girl, who's thirteen,

scratches his balls and yawns. He moved up here
to get away from civilisation
he says – from Babylon. He's buried his guns
down the yard. Another mound of biker stirs

and Carol creeps upstairs as John explains
how, strategically, you're better up a hill,
now we're close to the end of everything
when only the fittest, best armed will remain

to perpetuate the race. Three smart kids
file in in Sunday best; a shirt and tie
for the boy and floral dresses for the girls.
They breakfast on cornflakes and orange juice.

Their dad will take them to the Kingdom Hall
at nine. He doesn't live here anymore.
We joke with them. They smile indulgently.
We know they know that we are going to hell.

Trouble taking off

Alex has been to see the head-doctor
this morning. They had a nice long chat
about the blackouts and the episodes
and glass and why things always end

in tears, and the head-doctor asked Alex
to think
        very hard
                    about how he related to
the people around him, not just friends
or family but to people generally

and it isn't easy.
                 It isn't easy to think
that hard on an LC 350
power-valve Yamaha doing eighty-five
through thick traffic, skimming back

and forth across slick white lines,
clipping wing mirrors, carving up cars,
while all the time the reflective shades
you sport, instead of a visor,

funnel the wind right into your eyeballs
so that everything is blurred and indistinct,
and head-doctors know absolutely fuck all
about what it takes to concentrate

at ninety-eight on a blind bend
where one miscalculated twitch could
send you straight through a windscreen
or skittering under the wheels of an artic.

And Alex has been thinking so hard
that when the siren starts he's shocked,
slows down right away, without a chase
and pulls into the first lay-by.

By the time the cop has adjusted his cap
in the car window,
Alex has hung his helmet on the clocks,
tousled his hair, turned the ignition off,

straightened his specs and waits,
still astride the machine,
chewing his bottom lip.
                                    Now, son.
Having trouble getting airborne?

And Alex makes a piggy face,
tries to think of something witty,
feels a trace of a flush on his chalky skin
and mutters something completely incoherent.

You want your head testing, lad.

I've just bin.

A foul-tempered exchange, a flurry of documents,
a car door slamming and the copper's gone.
Alex puts his helmet back on,

takes the next left turn and bubbles
along for a few gentle miles then
buries the needle in the red line,
rips the throttle wide open.

Sea Monsters

Up from the pitsaw they are bringing fresh green boards.
At the window, hand over knotty hand, men pass them in;
each will season for a year. Rain scours the courtyard
as women hurry back and forth in heavy oilskin

capes and hoods. An apprentice shivers by the stable.
The stink of tanning hides wafts down the passageway
from the upholsterer's shop. I will make a table
next. A table so finely jointed, polished and inlaid

it will be a masterpiece. Out on the causeway,
sea serpents attack a cart. Men beat them off with staves.
A comet showed its lustrous tail last night. Some prayed.
Down the coast, another town is ravaged by the plague.

Stranded in Sub-Atomica

After four years of wrangling over unpaid rent, the housing co-op,
    the one he helped found
in the seventies, obtained an eviction order and repossessed.
    He went, owing thousands,
back to Sussex, where his mum and dad cleared out upstairs,
    aired his old bed
and, despite the disruption to their twenty-year routine, made him
    as welcome as they could.

Vic and Jill, who followed him into the flat, had to hire a skip
    to shift the shit he'd left.
There were piles of comics, old newspapers with articles circled,
    some with pages hacked out –
behind the settee the missing pieces, filed in cornflake packets –
    a pamphlet biography
of Rosa Luxemburg, copies of *Green Anarchist*, assorted tracts
    from the WRP,

A Nietzsche Reader, stacks of PG Tips boxes which leaked residue
    like bracken spores
when moved and gave a deep brown dusting to the work tops
    and the grease-caked floor.
At the back was an exercise bike, unused, and supermarket bags
    stuffed with paper and rags
and heaped waist high and supermarket bags full of rubbish and more
    supermarket bags.

His parents watched him eat his meals and hide behind *The Times*.
     Attempts at communication
tailed off into embarrassed silence then mum and dad held hands as he
     retired to the bedroom.
The flat stank and there were insects, insect larvae, wood-lice and slugs.
     Jill went down the shops
to buy disinfectant, rubber gloves, heavy-duty bin liners and bleach.
     For ten hours, non-stop,

they sifted, sorted through and binned his worldly goods. He sat
     and stared across the Downs
waiting for dark. There was a record player which worked, except that
     the speakers were blown,
and clothes among the rubbish, which seeped onto the clothes, and more
     rubbish in the cupboards
and mouse crap on the cooker and there were notes, scribbled notes –
     endless scribbled notes –

minutes of meetings that detailed who said what to whom, on what night
     and what they really meant,
drafts of letters of complaint, accusations to associates of unspecified slights,
     filed but never sent
and character assassinations of everyone he knew, presumably for reference.
     In short, documents
recording every nuance of his descent into paranoia and indifference
     were bagged and burnt.

By midnight, all that remained were lousy carpets, a table, two chairs
    and on the back wall,
in coloured marker pen and thick wax crayon, lines, loops and patterns,
    messages scrawled
in an erratic hand, drawings of people labelled with their names and crimes,
    broken hearts,
runes, animals, misquotes from the *Tao*. A cross between a Venn diagram
    and an astrologer's chart

it described the universe revolving round, set in a childish yellow sun,
    a giant ME.
Vic went to the car to fetch the wine and glasses, brushes and emulsion.
    In Sussex, he
shrank back into his chair as the moon was covered up by heavy cloud.
    The couple viewed
the mural for a while, traced the lines with finger tips, then set to work
    painting it out.

In Sub-Atomica, the princess struggled in the clutches of the arch-fiend
    Doctor Doom
and Johnny Storm – the Human Torch – threw himself into the fray against
    the villain's goons,
hurling balls of fire. He must reverse the evil Doctor's shrinking-ray
    or be marooned
forever. Somewhere outside Brighton, dawn's first light was filtering
    into an empty room.

Circus of the Self

I suppose it was almost unavoidable,
after Freud – hindsight is a handy tool –
that we should turn our gaze inwards.
Monkeys, lions, dancing bears and llamas

have long since ceased to astonish us.
The plate spinners and the high wire walkers
are inscrutable, the clowns anonymous.
Nowadays we like our pratfalls

figurative and savage. Our ringmasters
are Jerry, Graham, Tricia, Montel Williams.
(Esther Rantzen's a spectacle in her own right.)
We settle down and ooh and aah each night

at people just like us – but worse.
At my daughter's wedding I took it up the arse
on the lawn. Momma stole mah man. My brothers
stole mah man. I am married to an horse.

Chainsaw

Simon Armitage has his own chainsaw,
a bobby-dazzler with a bright orange flex.
He uses it to cut his pampas grass down
every year, which does rather suggest

he's never had to struggle up a bank side
laden like a mule with canthook, tool-kit,
hammer, wedges, fuel and a Husqvarna
262, through brash up to his armpits

until he's found the face and had a fag,
watched the rising sun, stripped to the waist
and yo-yoed the saw into crackling life.
Or stamped down the leaf litter at the base

of a hundred-and-twenty-foot Douglas fir,
smelt cat piss and turps from the day's first cut
and felt the hungry saw pull, trimming up.
I can't think he's checked the sweep of the butt

and the lean of the pole before he carved the gob.
And he won't have fought the gyroscopic thrust
of the engine and juddering Oregon chain
or snatched his lever, shouldered up and pushed

as the tree sat back, grabbed hammer and wedge
and heard the valley echo with the ring
of steel on steel and felt his muscles knot
and the tree yield as he drove the wedge right in.

I'll hazard he hasn't heard the creaking hinge
and rushing air as six tons of timber and branch
came roaring, like a train crash, to the ground.
And done this ten or twelve times before lunch.

I don't suppose he's set his bar in a stump vice,
straddled the baking saw, sun on his back
and stroked with a three-sixteenths round file
to make each cutter bright and sharp, in fact

I bet his teeth are black where all the chrome's
peeled off. I bet his chain is slack and blunt.
Yeah, Armitage has a glorified hedge trimmer
and he thinks it's a chainsaw.

The Golden Boys

These are the gilded lads in tweeds and cord,
with Dan Dare hair and lustrous brogues,
who vault into their sports cars with a wave.
They give a toot and speed away toward
some notional future. They'll misbehave,
of course, but are more loveable than rogue.

They never, after all, forget a birthday; just
to send the present or the card or telephone
and isn't forgetfulness part of their charm?
It's only when the real girls come, to dust
and chatter, break the spell, disturb the calm,
these evanescent princes are dethroned.

From exile, though, it isn't long before
they're summoned up again, by Bell's, on bright,
Haze-scented afternoons, glimpsed from windows
carrying flowers. They never reach the door
but flutter at the edge of sight. Their shadows
must be exorcised by Seroxat each night.

Heartbreak Hotel

Down at the end of Denmark St,
past the shops chock full of Strats,
of Marshall amps, Les Pauls, SGs
and music by the rack,

in each of which a sad-eyed
adolescent mangles 'Purple Haze'
and pony-tailed assistants wince
at every note he plays,

where roadies collect cabs for bands,
return them when they've wrecked them,
and dreamers ask to try that Gretsch
then only buy a plectrum;

past the bookers who audition
teen narcissists for pop videos;
past the wannabe DJs who strut
in stupid hats and baggy clothes;

yeah, there at the end of Denmark St
some joker's stuck a jobcentre.
It's rammed to the roof with proper jobs
but no one,
            not a one of us,
                    will ever stoop to enter.

In the Prospect of Whitby after the Private View

Two faaz'n years of culchah, Mickey Nails
complains and snorts into his beer. He gazes
balefully off down the greasy Thames
as the last charter boat plods its way upriver.

Water laps around the balcony piles. Astrid says
she *tought zat some of it vas good.* We all
agree the painting of the Black and Tan was nicely made.
Astrid liked the shed of vegetable tools

but Mickey thinks the avant-gardists' aspirations
far out-stripped their talent or ability
to just get out of bed. The self-harmer stroke
performance artist's photographs of cuts

looked superficial and did not impress us.
Harry Fink points out that he has raised much
better welts on Shel the crack-whore's arse
while making S&M home movies

and, come to think of it, she made a mess of his.
Then he gets maudlin because his artistic
output is currently being perused by the Met
and not with a view to sponsoring the work.

In fact, they're sniffing round the Pepys estate
to see if all the girls were really volunteers.
When the free pop ran out we came in here,
flush with cash, for more imported lager,

having done a roaring trade in substance
with the goateed wonders in the old tobacco warehouse
on Wapping Wall. It's laughable:
for all the yuppie dockside lofts, the City rich

barred up behind their electronic gates,
who glide like ghosts, in silver BMWs
and Mercs, the mile or so to work, the Prospect
still fills up with scum and arty hangers-on,

like us, in just the way it's always done. We leave.
The Bangladeshi kids, out on the cobbled street,
stop their football game to stare at us. They stare
as though we're aliens from space,

well dressed but walking, coked up and talking
too much and too fast and heading upstream
to see what the city has to offer.
Oh yeah, two thousand years of culture.

Same but Different

She blows her too-cool alto jazz down Villiers Street;
a minidisc and Peavey amp provide a lazy backbeat,
the swish of brush on snare and slap of bass repeat
as she shakes her California hair and taps her pretty feet

and up from the Embankment, with the river breeze,
come the crowds of well heeled Yanks and Japanese,
Eurostudes and backpackers on gap years from degrees
who fill her cap with coins that pay her music college fees.

Meanwhile, in Scarborough's faux-brutalist precinct,
a fat bloke with a Casio is kicking up an awful stink
and mutilating standards to the *tish-plink, tish-plink*
of a four-four Latin preset. The milling shoppers blink

and move away, not that he minds or even sees;
his eyes roll blank as billiard balls. He sweats and heaves
into 'Delilah'. It's the same. Really. The only difference is
the pittance in his keyboard case will go to local charities.

Not the Whitsun Weddings

I was in good time but they were late, the Stags,
    and filtered on,
some hefting rucksacks, some Adidas bags,
in odds and sods. Even after London
had jerked into reverse, while I arranged
and rearranged my things repeatedly
(to guard the double airline seat I'd won),
I saw the coach's demographic change
as they moved on, with cool authority,
whole families who vacated looking stunned.

The Stags, though not discreet and not polite,
    were not quite rude.
You knew you wouldn't want to pick a fight
with them but still they managed to exude
a sort of *bonhomie,* tinged with menace.
They'd just annexed the whole half-carriage,
my seats excepted, when I heard a squawk
which indicated they had found the Hennies
heading north, then, like a failing marriage,
the train eased to a halt at Finsbury Park.

It hung in aching heat, among black bricks,
        the journey stalled
above the bagel shops and ticket office.
In daylight, on the bowling alley wall,
a neon tenpin flickered like a loss
and silence fell along the crowded car.
We didn't know but further up the line
the 12:45 out of King's Cross
had jumped the rails approaching Potters Bar.
Suspension groaned: the linkage whined

and we moved off again on creaking joints:
        the tannoy coughed
and spoke: we waddled over shifting points,
through baking suburbs listening to the soft,
unworldly Geordie burr announcing that
something untoward but comfortingly vague
had sent us shuttling over Hertfordshire.
Soon though, the carriage buzzed with bawdy chat;
the Stags had spread out like a laddish plague
infecting all the coach with noise and beer

and I looked round to find the tables strewn,
    a jubilee
of tinnies, all the luggage racks festooned
with photocopies of the groom-to-be's
bare arse. The Stags slipped into rugby shirts
blazoned with the legend *Kibble's Big One*
and while the best man brandished a camcorder
the bolder souls went up the coach to flirt
with Hens they hoped might easily be conned
by pettifogging princes of disorder.

The Hennies played it dumb-but-sly and soaked
    the flattery up.
They sniggered at the boastful, half-cut blokes
and secretly decided who'd get tupped
that night. Non-combatants looked on aghast
as groom-to-be pulled on a dress and stalked
the corridor in drag, Lord of Misrule,
dispensing grog to people as he passed.
We stopped to take on alcohol at York,
the late-arriving, steel-shod Ship of Fools.

Mobiles bleated here and there – relatives
        concerned about
our health but no one in the coach could give
a damn. The Stags had broke the absinthe out
and everything got cloudy; countryside
passed by, a sort of green and yellow smear.
The train, a moral vacuum, was aswarm
with pheromones which hurtled to collide.
Two satyrs rapped on safety glass and leered
at Durham schoolgirls on the platform

who looked away embarrassed and confused.
        And gathering speed
once more we flew, the air perfumed with booze
and latent sex, past Berwick-upon-Tweed
like some absurd prenuptial carnival
for unions that may or may not last,
till, with a shriek of dissipating power
the party ground into the terminal.
In Edinburgh, where partygoers mass,
they staggered off, an utter bloody shower.

Landcrab

Alec Issigonis's greatest design, the Austin 1800
www.landcrab.net

Once they ruled the earth, these primitive things,
these crude things seen now only in scrapyards
or tarpaulined in urban front gardens,
never-finished projects waiting to be passed
from optimist to dreamer and then last,
their tyres perished, wiring looms hardened
to brittleness, delivered to the scrapyard
anyway, all cracked lamps and dented wings.

There was a time, though, when half the country
went to work in one or something like it,
when early morning roads rang to the clash
of pressed-steel toolboxes hoisted into their
capacious boots, with bradawls, saws, set squares,
and spirit levels slung in in canvas bags,
the spanners, Whitworth, A/F and metric,
chiming out a pre-dawn cacophony.

At night, in country lanes and cul-de-sacs,
the springs of football field-wide back seats creaked
as, in a mess of pants and Pretty Pollys,
every second citizen was got;
and Britain's favourite flutter then was not
the Lotto but getting them through MOTs.
Brakes were bodged, sills gobbered up out in the street
by sweating oily men sprawled on their backs.

But now these automotive curate's eggs
are rarely featured in nostalgic art.
Loaded blokes don't rate them up near sex,
Jeremy Clarkson can or will not love them,
soccer stars and models are above them
and Jay Kay from Jamiraquai collects
Ferraris, but, in truth, the better part
of that young man ran down his mother's leg.

It Lives!

In one gruesome experiment, it seems,
they, with their habitual disregard for
public safety, took the mind of a pig,

implanted it in the body of a pig,
dressed it up in a cheap suit, furnished it
with a full set of opinions and let it loose.

For over eighteen months they monitored
its every move, kept tabs on its contacts
and administered the stabilising drugs,

as necessary, when it slept. Before long,
though, it became clear that they were not
in control at all. They lost track of it

for days on end. The team of specialists
would arrive at the staked-out café to see
a kitchen door flap, an informant shrug

and hear the bins clatter in the next alley.
It has been spotted holding forth in bars
as far apart as Hemel Hempstead, Poole

in Dorset and Hebden Bridge, sometimes
on the same night. In May they thought
they had it, at a Travelodge off the M6

but when the Mondeo door creaked open,
to the orchestrated crash of cocking guns,
a corpulent rep stepped into the spotlights

and crapped himself. While it is at liberty
no woman, man or child can sleep safely.
They will take no responsibility and despite

all evidence to the contrary, all the horror
and fear they have brought into the world,
have begun to deny that it even exists.

Goodbye Yellow Brick Road

We vault over the barrier and scramble
down the bank. Our boots are soaked with dew,
our clothes spattered with mud and torn by brambles.
The headlights leach the battery as the bonnet
spews out steam. The car will stay there, slewed
and stuck, up on the verge, till traffic cops
find time to slap a Police Aware sign on it
and, later, send a truck to haul it off.

There'll be no search. Nobody knows we're gone.
A trawl of Swansea's all they can afford.
Staff levels as they are, they'll just send forms
to flop among the circulars and bills
and get thrown out. We're strictly off the record,
left no forwarding address, unencumbered
by possessions, heading, nameless, for the hills.
Erased, rubbed out, we are not even numbers.

We avoid the roads, return to the farm
and find that it's a ruin. The animals
have fled to the edges of the wood. The barn
is wrecked, its roof caved in. Disconsolate,
the cattle bawl, reluctantly feral.
We skirt the village, weave across an orchard,
pop a window, steal dry socks and chocolate,
make tea and toast and leave by the back yard.

The moor's awash with shifting cloud. I take
your red, raw hands. Your face is beautiful.
Your cheeks are pink. It is too cold to speak.
We've got the gun and nearly forty rounds
and food and know we are invulnerable –
that nothing matters now, or can go wrong.
The whip of wind, footsteps in sodden ground,
the blistering rain. This is our love song.

Getting in Touch with our Feminine Sides

It's morning and it's just the two of us
in the Transit crew-bus, driving out to work
past dew-hung spruce, in this neck of the woods.
    The floor is strewn

with chainsaws, chains, tools, grease-guns, tubes of grease
while the whole van stinks of sap and two-stroke mix.
I would screw my oil-stained Maxproof coat up
      into a ball

and try to grab some kip but today I just can't sleep.
And it's not the jolting over pot-holed roads
or the flare of light that's keeping me awake –
    I'm worried sick.

Geoff is smoking pre-rolled Holborn roll-ups
by the barrow-load. He flicks the oily butts
out of the narrow window slit and says,
      frankly, not much.

The towering Sitka spin by, blue and gorgeous
in the warmth of the brilliant, early morning sun
and it's all so picturesque that I am overcome
      with a desire

to unburden, to share. So I brace myself and say:
Here, kid.   *What's thu want?*
I think I might have got me girlfriend pregnant.
        There. I did it.

He changes down a gear, furrows his brow,
sucks once on his rolly and then speaks:
It's nowt clever, lad. Rats do it every six weeks.
        I was hoping

for something a little more reflective,
some empathy, a sympathetic ear perhaps,
but you have to admit it puts things
        in perspective.

My Body is Contemptible

His faith in obsolete technology was touching.
The care with which he tensioned the cable,
adjusted the finely machined rods,
attended to the springs and cork pads
of his eight-leading-shoe front brake, moving.

It's a switch, our lad, his brother said.
It's how you set 'em up, he replied
with the air of a Shaolin adept and polished
the alloy cowl. On the downhill right hander,
past the start-finish, on the second lap,

his front wheel locked. His wrist broke
on impact and his kneecap smashed but it was
the Matchless behind that cracked his pelvis
and burst his spleen. Marshals waved
gaily with their red flags, glad to be part

of the action at last. The St. John's crew
creaked into life like Disney vultures, squeezed
him, a pallid daddy-long-legs, from his leather
suit and strapped him in the back of their
ambulance. Linda took the car and we,

once it was confirmed that he could still
swear, got ready for the next race. By the end
of the season he was shuffling around the pits
on crutches, whining about his plates and the pain
and saying, *Perhaps we've underrated Triumph frames.*

The Toerag Situationists

They robbed our lass's Astra GTi in Middlesbrough.
It reappeared next day, bonnet removed by bolt-cropper,
stripped of wheels, seats, inlet manifold and wing mirrors.

The stereo was gone and every one of her cassettes,
except, propped on the dashboard, *Elton John: The Greatest Hits.*
And I read in the news that they'd cleaned a warehouse out;

a hundred and fifty thousand pounds' worth of CDs
in a single night, but what absolutely mystified the police
was why they'd sorted through them all and left the Bee Gees.

Johnny Cash

And the Lord spake unto my mam, sometime in the 1970s,
    and Yea he sayèd
Every home wherein there dwells a teenager, shall also have a record player.
    And this despite
a previous unhappy experience when they bought me, at the age of four,
    a copy of
'Hippy Hippy Shake' by the Swinging Blue Jeans, borrowed a Dansette
    then had to endure

endless afternoons of the same disc spun over and over, relieved only
    by Lonnie Donegan's
skiffle classic 'My Old Man's a Dustman' for an hour or two. I've thought
    of those days
lately while sitting with my nieces aged five and three as they watch *Toy Story*
    on video
for the thirty-seventh time and I've thought of the Barnes household
    in 1990

where, for six months, all activity was accompanied by the the strains
    of Aled Jones,
We're walking in the air issuing from the VCR, *The Snowman*,
    an ill-considered
Christmas gift for the boy Ivan. The record player was soon regretted too.
    It looked
innocuous enough, a GEC with wood finish surround and speakers
    and a lift-off

plastic lid that doubled as a prison cell for cats and other small mammals.
 Soon though,
the house began to fill with Led Zeppelin records, Yes, for Christ's sake, and even
 Atomic Rooster –
though never, never ever, Genesis. The very next birthday I received a pair
 of stereo
headphones so that I could twitch and flick to 'Interstellar Overdrive' alone,
 at any time of day.

But this was not enough for Ruby Shirley Turnbull. She retaliated by buying
 two Johnny Cash records
and a Jim Reeves double album, then refusing to learn how to work the deck.
 Holiday afternoons
I'd just be slipping *The Dark Side of the Moon* onto the turntable
 and she'd appear
at the living room door. *Don't be putting that rubbish on. Let's have Johnny Cash,*
 she'd say.

We'd have a row. She'd win. I'd set the disc up and she'd go and peel carrots
 in the kitchen
where she couldn't hear it. I used to hate Country & Western so much, like,
 it made my ears bleed.
Years later though I heard 'Folsom Prison Blues' coming out of my bedsit radio.
 Oh crap. I thought,
He says more about life in one song than Jon Anderson could in a career's-worth
 of turgid,

gatefold concept albums and this is sharper and funnier than anything the Pink,
  joyless bloody
Floyd ever managed to produce. I tried to imagine Cash at a Led Zeppelin gig –
  Hey there, boy.
The song seems to have remained the same for about twenny minutes now
  an' if it don't
change soon I'm gunna ram that violin bow up yure ass – saadways.
  And Jimmy Page

may have been as hard as nails when faced with a 26" Ferguson
  and a hotel window
but I suspect he'd have shuffled off stage a broken man at this remonstration.
  Which leads me
to the sad conclusion, as so often in my life, that all that adolescent self-assertion
  was in vain.
Me mam was right again. *My name is Sue. How do you do?* My name is Tim,
  Johnny, and things are looking grim.

Language Barrier

The decorators can't say terracotta.
Like a South Sea tribe who only have one word
for blue and green and will not recognise
the delicate gradations in between.

They take the swatch and look at it
and look at her and look at it again
and write the Dulux number down
and say: *We'll get a can of brown, then*

for the lounge

Lullaby for an Alcoholic

Put down your head and flutter into troubled sleep.
Dream parachuting soldiers yanked across the sky

on sudden winds. Fall into darkness, bored on trains
by blethering strangers, or in your bed as from the street

a fire engine dopplers past. Pull up the gritty sheets
and count a million sheep or more. Imagine waves

exploding on the pier or make a mental picture
of a silent kite cartwheeling down an empty beach.

Wake up on a sofa-bed, a silver curry tray
set on the floor, a coat wrapped tight about your head.

Surface from beneath an unfamiliar eiderdown,
a warm body beside you and the stink of sweat and sex

or stir in a dusty meadow on a summer afternoon
and lick your lips and catch a little sour taste of death.

Whoops

The beer makes him talkative
and weepy.
He clutches Caroline's
chubby fingers in his own
calloused paws

and tells her
how much he still loves her;
how, in truth,
she was the only girl,
and there had been many,
the only girl
he ever really loved.
She gives a weak smile,
having heard it all
a thousand times before.

A table away, his bride
of three months,
the girl he brought here
from New Zealand,
looks on, damp-eyed
and slack-jawed.

A grand piano topples
from a skyscraper window.
The old pit shaft opens
under the weight of the horse

The Stockman's Calendar: Four Northern Æclogues

Spring

The fields fill up with fresh green grass and beasts, just recently released,
    who kick their heels in skittish dances.
Songbirds warble up the Eden valley, stake out their claims to territory
    balanced on the tips of branches,

as I lie on my side and watch the Doctor Martens swagger off
    and when I move come rushing back.
Hormones and the rising of the sap are all that I can think
    provoked this unprovoked attack.

Summer

Frankie Valli issues from the disco as they leave. His shirt is stained with sweat.
    She's pretty in her summer dress.
The glass comes out of nowhere, smashes on his head and cuts his face and neck;
    the flying splinters make a mess

of hers. She will, of course, be scarred for life. The pissed-up thug is quickly caught
    and his defence is a novel one.
The night was hot, he tells the court, and in the failing light he thought
    the couple were from Bridlington.

Autumn

He lies back in the dried-up ditch, stares at the haws and the harvest moon,
    and listens to the sound of the car.
He sees the lights flash through the hedge and knows that they are after him
    with baseball bats and iron bars.

At 4 AM, he scrambles out and makes his dew-drenched way back home.
    Next year there is a big pub fight
and one of the gang gets killed. When he reads it he thinks it's sad but still
    it serves the stupid bastard right.

Winter

The car park puddles are filmed with ice. The chestnut twigs are clacking in
    a bitter wind from out the east
and they've been drinking all afternoon and aren't in the mood for packing in
    just because serving time has ceased.

Next day, not one of them can remember what happened to start the dispute
    but the doctor's skin was brown
so they drove like hell in hot pursuit, and gave him a taste of fist and boot
    when they caught him up at the edge of town.

Fish

We knew it was going to be a tough contract as soon as we saw
    the smug jumper,
the fussy little beard and the attaché case but what capped it all
    was the fish on the car.

It said that we, the undeserving, could be sacked, not for the usual
    breaches of discipline
or contravention of the Health and Safety at Work (1974)
    Act, or thieving

or failing to keep our vehicle's insurance and road tax up to date
    but at his pious whim.
The fish on the car said we would be harassed, paid the minimum rate,
    get bollocked for coming in

even five minutes late, work till our legs and backs and shoulders ached,
    work, in short, like slaves
while he sat in a lay-by with his packed lunch and Phil Collins tapes,
    sipping milky tea and waiting to be saved.

Services

In the bleak backwater that is the M4
corridor, we break for coffee and a rest.
Granada Granary or Little Chef's the best
on offer and it's uniformly poor.
The carvery woman in her corporate pinafore
looks listless; badly paid and badly dressed.
We wait around forever, unimpressed,
by service only slow not even sure.

She'd be better working in the village shop
serving folks she knows with milk and bread,
who've time to pass, to stop and maybe swap
the latest village gossip but instead
it's Trust House Forte pay her – not a lot –
here in the Land that Time and Motion Forgot.

We encounter something exotic but not on VHS

Moving site, our tatty little convoy
of tractors, vans and men and dogs
kicks up a storm of dirt. The County thrums
and pulses down the stony forest road.

Brian, forging on ahead, ear-muffed, oblivious,
rounds the bend first and sees them there –
buck naked, shameless naturists, as God
intended (but with training shoes and socks).

He thunders past the clearing then applies the brakes
and waits for us to catch him up. Pete nearly
crashes laughing, swinging on the Fordson
steering wheel. I crawl by in the Astra, assorted

mongrels smashing at the windows, yipping
at the startled nudists who stand stock still
like unattractive statues – blotchy, white
and pink and sagging in the oddest places.

A layer of limestone dust is settling on them.
I smirk and wave and one poor soul responds.
Much mirth ensues at bait time. Pete weeps tears
of purest joy. *That big bugger had nowt*

much to show off. It looked like a machine gun
poking through an hedge. Brian roars and rolls
about. The granny at the picnic table, legs
apart, he says, seemed to be feeding a badger.

This is the best thing to happen since the tit-
hanging video, or the bumper stash
of porn we found in bushes in the wood.
It's better even than when Brian's brother, who

is on the other bus, lent us (I say lent. He
didn't know we had it) the hardcore skinflick
with twenty-six blokes shagging in a circle.
This is better because they are real people;

real, ridiculous people we believed
existed only in the twilight zone
of access TV, Channel 4 documentaries,
H&E. They are perverts, we are normal,

we declare. Some of you will tell me that
the procreative act is sacred, not a side-show;
that the human form is to be cherished,
a thing of beauty, and that we demean

ourselves by treating sex as just another
circus stunt laid on for our entertainment,
sniggering like boys at tits and bums.
I say we're all going to die; do crap jobs

and die. Oh, and we revere Rabelais;
we, fat fingered oafs, fumble under skirts
and wallow in our fornication, drink
skins full, piss lakes and tremble with laughter.

In Brueghel paintings we hang hairy arses
out of windows, shit, then (coprophiles all)
inspect the stools for texture and for stink.
We rut like Zola's bulls and rude peasants

and beauty does not enter it. Around us,
wrens, flies and polecat-ferrets go at it.
We sniff the air and savour the reek;
neither delicacy nor intellect

are welcome here. Birth and copulation
and death. They'll do for us, old chum. No
higher purpose needed here, my friend.
No Quakerish whimpering temples; no

wracks of Catholic guilt. We are gristle
and muscle and bone. We just are and, well,
we'll rot soon enough; but be assured,
clothed or unclothed, ours will inherit the earth.

New Romantic

Sometimes the world's so full of silly clutter
it seems to be just scenery and props
for some bad play; the dialogue is mutter,
the actors in it merely hams and fops.

On other, brighter days the sense of utter
desolation lifts, the penny drops
and it strikes me that we're all in the gutter
but some of us are gazing at the shops.

Revolutionary Art

This is the one, then. The first great work of art of the new millennium.
A conceptualist masterpiece as audacious in its scale as in its execution.

Rachel Whiteread will turn puce and spit feathers when she hears of it;
the Chapmanbrothers-Hirst-Ofili-Lucas-Emin Axis have a hissy fit.

It makes that bloke in Hoxton who is shredding all his pants and chairs
and fridge look pretty feeble. And best of all it's made by amateurs,

naïve artists who haven't heard of Goldsmiths or Central St. Martins,
hirsute enthusiasts who, it's safe to say, will never visit Tate Modern

but who challenge our notions of what art is and force us to question
what it's for. They are worthy heirs to the Dadaist anti-tradition,

bold in their unconventional choice of tools and site and techniques,
daring in their use of rocket launchers, tanks and gelignite. They speak

volumes about faith, truth, culture, death and man's inhumanity to man.
Centuries hence art lovers will gaze in awe on the empty vaults at Bamiyan.

Succubus

How much stranger love is
than he could imagine. She fills
his answerphone with abuse so shrill
it's barely comprehensible.

She leaps from a neighbour's garden
and drags him squawking into the way
of the W3; the bite marks on his nose
and cheek are visible for days.

The bus shrieks and shudders
to a halt. The police are called.
His house is glazed with hardboard.
Rubbish covers his lawn,

graffiti, his walls. Love, it seems,
is two parts terror to one part despair.
You can't shake hands and call it a draw.
You can't just declare

because love follows you home at night.
It's skulking in the shadows there.
It lifts tiles and rattles window frames.
Love electrifies the air.

Wogs

In the Ziznivy Pes, some dickhead from the Prague Post
orders my girlfriend to keep an eye on his bag and coat.
Watch 'em your fucking self, you dickhead, she says.
Sorry, doll. He explains, *It's just I thought you were Czech.*

Later on, a huge, pissed-up U.S. Marine strips off his shirt
and tells us how U.S. Marines are the best troops in the world
and offers everybody out – one at a time or all at once.
None of the drinkers (English, Russian, German, French) responds.

That night a pair of gypsies stop some American guy,
who's alone in Namesti Republiky Metro, and ask the time.
He looks at his watch and wakes up stabbed and robbed.
Next afternoon, the joyful word gets round in Josefov.

While we await the northward creep of ninety million
Mexicans, the stretching of supply lines and the slow erosion,
the steady chipping away time performs on all empires, it seems
we must content ourselves with futile little gestures such as these.

Shoot

This is a film set,
furnished with what's known,
in that laddish argot, as wall-to-wall fanny.

Models, half-dressed
or draped in overcoats
and clutching cups of sweet, black coffee,

clump to and fro.
The High and Mighty boys, serene
giraffes with good skin and strong jaws,

remain unmoved.
At the centre of it all
three youths, generic disco extras,

ooze hormones
and, dumb with wonder
like eager, eighteenth century anatomists,

pore over
a Pirelli calendar.
The real girls might just as well not exist.

Later in the day,
one of the these young bucks
spots the Alpha Babe leaving a changing room,

calculatedly
flustered, smoothing her frock.
He leans towards me in the backstage gloom.

That, he confides,
has got my name written
all over it. I snort. He gets in a flounce

and looks like
he's sipping cabbage juice.
Why so glum when the all world is yours, my Prince?

9/11

The first I hear of it is in the butcher's shop.
Tom and his customer stand there gazing up
at the ghettoblaster hanging from a meathook.
They've flown a bloody plane into a tower block.

I imagine a light aircraft, Cessna, accident.
The old fella leans on his stick, says he went
gladly last time and he'd gladly go again.
I scuff the sawdust, draw on the sticky scent

of fat and blood and buy some steak for tea.
Puzzled, back home, I put the telly on.
Sometimes we walk round staring at our feet,
look up and find we're where we started from.

Sick Again

You are searching for a missing piece of jigsaw,
like a kid that's lost its mother in the big store
or an apeman who is scratching with a pig jaw,
unsure exactly, what it is you dig for.

What was that?

Through a whitewashed courtyard bleached by inappropriate,
    nearly Mediterranean sun
then stoop into a musty junkshop presided over by the
    murderer Christie and Ma Broon.
The rooms have a whiff of elderly relations visited on summer
    Sunday afternoons
with Mack Sennett shorts on the telly, cold pork for tea and, for
    afters, butterfly buns.

Move into the makeshift shrine, all glass cases stuffed with
    papers, scrapbooks, photographs,
film posters, pairs of bowlers and bow ties and the actual *Sons of
the Desert* hats,
and here's some correspondence with a fan, bedridden since her
    unexplained collapse
but delighted they could find the time, and Stan, sick and old
    and tired in a late on-set snap,

bitter since the studio took the writing off his hands, and Ollie
    looking fat, even for him, and used.
Cramp into the makeshift picture-house; a room with a big TV
    and salvaged Wesleyan pews,
where Ma loads a cassette and off you go – *Scram, Blockheads,
Laughing Gravy, One Good Turn*
and, best of all, *Big Business*. Watch the stupid escalating war
    with boggle-eyed James Finlayson

where they take turns to wreck his house as he wrecks their car
    and the crowd troop back and forth
and forth and back and the cop double-takes. Writhe and hoot
    with laughter, shake with mirth
at the pie in the face, a hoof in the rump, a poke in the eye,
    Sartre in Africa, a scissored-off tie,
the flaming thumb, firestorm on the Ruhr, marines with Zippo
    lighters strolling through My Lai,

Oppenheimer quoting the *Bhagavad-Gita,* saying *I am become*
    death; destroyer of worlds, a horse
on a piano that makes you laugh until you gasp for air and,
    lastly, hear the music. It's 'The Cuckoo Waltz'.

The touring Shakespeare company's visit is eagerly awaited in Grozny in 1953

One is told that the Russians now disapprove of tragedy,
and there was a performance of Hamlet *in the Turk-Sib region*
which the audience decided spontaneously was a farce.
William Empson, *Some Versions of Pastoral*, 1935.

Shamil still remembers the original
in twenty-four. "It was hilarious.
Ha ha ha – *Po-lon-yus up his arras.*
That gawky kid in the sketch with the skull
and big misunderstanding with the girl –
Go and live, dirty bitch, in a nun's house.
I laughed from when we saw the silly ghost
right to the fight when all the fools get killed."

This comedy sustained him through, he says,
famine and forced collectivisation,
the NKVD terror and the purges.
In the gulag it could still raise a grin.
He prays the Prince is played by Brian Rix
and thinks it can't get any worse than this.

Binary

Let us go to face extinction
somewhere by the sea, like Frinton,
Tenby, maybe, or, at worst,
in a bungalow on the Yorkshire coast.

We'll walk our old, arthritic dog
and watch him crap and tell him off
for balking at the absurd commands
we make believe he really understands

then drag him up the front and back.
We'll take a flask and matching macs,
a tartan rug to warm our knees
in seafront shelters, sheltered from the breeze.

On Sundays we'll eat cold roast ham
with salad or perhaps a can
of crabmeat or some Skipjack tuna,
so long as we can operate the opener –

It's stiffer than it used to be.
From deck chairs we'll gaze out to sea,
cursing as our powers wane
to wash the upstairs windows or unblock the drains.

But if we're lucky and we both last long enough,
we may just be redeemed by our sum of stored-up love.

The Men from U.N.C.O.O.L.

We had been sitting in the ICA
with free booze and fags and free canapés

served up by lazy girls from shiny trays;
free entertainment – two or free DJs,

spoken word shouted frew a shit PA.
It felt like we'd been there for firty days

and firty nights. It didn't so much as
stimulate us let alone arouse us –

the chicks with the lips and low slung trousers,
the guys with the glasses and the goatee fuzz –

so we scoffed the scallops, hopped on a bus
and headed back to the Jolly Butchers,

caught last orders, drank each other's health,
watched the wrestlers wrestling on the shelf,

considered how, if you are born to wealth,
you never need to part with your own gelt

and how we both, ironically, felt
beer tastes better when you bought it yourself.

God has a Day Off

And lo, it occurred to God that he hadn't had a minute's respite since that Sunday
    and all this omniscience
was doing his head in (knowing everything about everything, all the time, totally,
    it's worse than blue cheese
or chocolate for migraine) and he thought it might be nice to contemplate a Monet,
    a fish, a leaf or a plate of steak
and chips, on its own, for once, instead of the whole of creation throughout eternity.
    If he saw a doctor he knew
(for certain) he would say – *It's work-related stress. What you need is a holiday.*
    You can afford to take
a holiday? So God weighed up his options, gazed absent-mindedly into infinity
    and threw a sicky.

Bored with transcending gender, race and whatever, he manifested himself as a whey-
    faced bloke with a lisp,
(a great long streak of pelican piss in a shabby suit, tie in his pocket), got up early,
    went down Smithfield
Market where the bars are open at five and had a pint of Stripe – *Can't waste the day*
    in bed, he thought,
savouring the cool, sweet/sour lager as butchers in bloody aprons, all jowl and belly
    and beef, came and went
and in the corner fellas buzzing with drugs and up to no good, though hard to say
    exactly what and God
realised he couldn't say exactly what, just he had a feeling and they looked shifty
    and later that morning

at Grange-over-Sands, watching oyster catchers on the mudflats in Morecambe Bay
  he tried to imagine,
found he could only imagine, the lines and arcs of stones arranged by that Goldsworthy
  chap to make his art,
now buried deep in silt and out of sight. Stopping for a drink in Cork around midday
  he found a street of pubs
and was moved by this sanguinity, then he ate meat loaf and turnip greens at a Tennessee
  truck stop where,
in the gift shop, a boy in a *Jesus is my Savior* tee-shirt pouted and began to bray –
  Wha's that man look funny,
mommy? Later on, in the Congo, a militiaman he met cursed injustice, France and poverty
  then bought God a Coke.

Now God lives in a caravan outside Newquay and some trust funds he established pay
  the bills and every day
he takes a stroll down to the beach where he reads novels and finds he's not entirely
  out of step with Nietzsche.

What?

What? she protests, outraged, palms upturned, *What?*
It's the default response when you've been caught,
a spasm, a tic, a nearly neural reflex,

but, as well, a rune, a charm, a magic word,
a key for the gateway to another world
where there is no cause and there are no effects.

Archie Rice with everything

The fat comedian's looking rather smug.
He's on a roll. He's just done Tony Blair
and wanking, mobile phones and Class B drugs
in nine minutes flat – and they lapped it up.
He dabs his brow, slicks back his oily hair
and, with a sparkle in his eyes, erupts:

McDonald's checkout kids are all as thick
as shit. Where the fuck do they get the staff?
Pizza-faced, illiterate, robotic
and every one's as ugly as it's rude.
He pauses, leaves a hole for them to laugh
then bawls: *You know they spit in people's food?*

Outside the club, the drizzle's turned to sleet.
The burger joint looks welcoming and warm.
The floors are clean; the kids are pretty neat
and have acquired certain social skills,
it's fair to judge from seeing him perform,
our friend the paunchy comic never will –

who nibbles on a fry and licks his lips
and tries to picture, maybe, young Anish
aged fifty-five and retired as he slips
into a Merc and guns it to the Med
or one-star Joe who joins the *presque riche*
exploiting his small gifts to get ahead.

Next night, the walk-in-wardrobe cum pissoir
that passes for a Dressing Room in Leeds
is full of smoke. The clown hacks up catarrh
and half his lunch, a martyr to his nerves
and the peptic ulcer stomach acid feeds.
He prays we get the fare that we deserve.

Love isn't ...

I

Sadism is not a hobby. No. Sadism is not
twanking someone's arse until they shout

Elephant! Sadism is not nailing your mate's
dick to a plank no matter how much it makes

him squeak and trill with the pain. It is not
a lifestyle choice. It is not a rubber suit

or a uniform you can slip on, weekends,
down Madam Fru Fru's Cellar of Torments

for a few hours' relaxation. It is a worm
in the brain. It is a second skin that's worn

under your own, that chafes until you wince.
It's the bitter gift of X-ray vision or prescience.

It is a virus, a pathogen, particular to you,
infecting everything you see or think or do.

II

Masochism is, I realise
in a moment of lucidity,
merely a highly specialised
sub-category of stupidity.

The Radioactive Kid

Why do you write the way you write? he asks,
nods and adds, in case there was any doubt,
I mean, you know, it's dark. I sigh, relax
and leave him. I'm back at Stainmore, thumb out,

the end of April 1986,
nithered, shivering, hair plastered to face,
boots soaking up the groundwater like wicks,
rain pouring down my shirt-neck in cascades

and each raindrop plutonium enriched.
My pelt drank it in through every pore,
irradiating the gruel-thin blood which
carried the poison to my very core

and there the change began – cells were ruptured,
DNA strands unfurled, reformed reversed,
gradually, painfully, restructured –
that left me whole but with this three-fold curse:

a sense, half wonderstruck and half appalled,
that something dreadful's about to happen,
a compulsion to tell and, above all,
the sure knowledge that no one will listen.

Notes

Chainsaw
Simon Armitage's 'Chainsaw versus the Pampas Grass' can be found in *The Universal Home Doctor* (Faber and Faber, 2002).

Getting in Touch with our Feminine Sides
The Sitka spruce is the major commercial conifer in Britain.

Heartbreak Hotel
Cabs, in this context, are speaker cabinets not taxis.

My Body is Contemptible
A Matchless is a venerable British racing bike.

Sea Monsters
Used for cutting lengths of timber, a pitsaw is an old-fashioned two-man handsaw operated with one person standing above the log while the other works (in a pit) below.

We encounter something exotic but not on VHS
The County mentioned in the first stanza is a four-wheel drive Ford tractor much used for timber extraction in the forestry industry. A Fordson is a Fordson Super Major – a classic tractor of the 1960s.

Also Available from Donut Press

Boys' Night Out in the Afternoon, by Tim Wells. £10 (plus £1 P&P)

What was that?, by Tim Turnbull. £5 (plus £1 P&P)

Buffalo Bills, by John Stammers. £5 (plus £1 P&P)

The Switch, by Jonathan Asser. £4 (plus £1 P&P)

Cheques, POs and IMOs payable to Donut Press.
Donut Press, PO Box 45093, London, N4 1UZ

www.donutpress.co.uk